Hide and Squeaks

Preface

A true story of a little girl trying to survive in a world
where hope is sometimes hard to find.

Acknowledgments

Thanks to our dear friends, Rusty, Verna, and Sylvia, who
have loved and supported us throughout this process.
Always there to listen, you gave wonderful advice.

We give special acknowledgment to Debbie Maddigan, who wrote Laura's
story first. *A Little Girl called Squeaks* is the adult version of Laura's life.
Thank you, Debbie, for doing all that hard work of getting Laura's story down
on paper. Your book has often been our reference point for Little Laura!

We also give special thanks to our financial supporters, who
were very generous with their gifts. Without their faith and trust
in us, we could not have moved forward with this book.

Dear Laura,

Meeting you was an astounding moment for us. You shone from within as you smiled and graciously thanked us for reading your first book.

It was hard to believe that the woman standing before us was once a lost, little girl. You grew up without the care of a mother and basically had to take care of yourself every day of your young life. You had to suffer so long without knowing that you are a significant person in this world. God has long since shown you how loved and valued you really are. We are honoured to bring your little girl story to our pages with colour and poetry. We are so humbled to be a part of this project that God has designed and ordained from the first day we met. You have the biggest heart. We know that your greatest dream is to make sure that by reading our book, hurting children in the world will know there is hope. If even one child is touched by the stories of your life, you will be happy. Thank you for sharing your "God Shots" with us!

Love,

Leslie and Lucy

My Story

I'll tell you the story of how my name came to be,
And how the name Squeaks was given to me.

Mom's friends heard me laugh in my little girl voice,
In these uncertain moments, I would squeak, not by choice.

I guess I was nervous, and tried to make light,
Of the times I met people who didn't seem right.

But no matter the day, no matter how sad,
There was always a sparkle of light to be had.

What I want you to know, what I want you to see,
Are the strong arms of God enveloping me.

I met some good people all through my life,
I could see He was working to ease all my strife.

So friends, as I share these dear stories of mine
Hold on to your own special memories that shine.

Hold them tight always, and close to your heart,
God has given them to you as a great place to start.

My Panda

Let's begin as you see me, alone in the dark.
No light could shine in; there were cracks in my heart.

I would hide in the corners, or under Mom's bed,
While I clutched onto Panda and laid down my head.

I was scared and afraid, wondering what I could say,
So my mom would not yell at me most of the day.

She brought many men home; it's those times I'd hide.
Those men sometimes touched me, and then I would cry.

As the stories go on, you'll see how I lived,
With my drug addict mom who had nothing to give.

I was so glad I had Panda, to hold onto tight,
I cuddled him each day and each long lonely night.

As I hugged him so tightly, somehow I knew,
That somebody loved me. It had to be true!

The World Outside my Window

Look up and you'll find me, at the window alone
Watching my pigeons on the ledge made of stone.

With Mom fast asleep, I could not make a sound;
If I did, she would yell, slap, or kick me around.

If Mom stayed asleep, I learned how to peek,
With the curtains around me, I would look at the street.

I met with the pigeons, who danced on the ledge,
We'd write clever songs, and to my birds, I would pledge:

"You're my forever friends; to you I'll be true,
You're in my heart; I'll not forget you.

So dance little pigeons, dance happily.
The world outside my window is where I am free!"

The Light of the Moon

My world became bigger when I ventured outside.
I'd leave our room when Mom's guests came inside.

When nighttime fell and I couldn't stay there,
I'd escape into the cool black night air.

I was just five years old, but I didn't feel scared;
At the glorious moon and the stars I would stare.

By squinting my eyes, I'd see twinkling stars form
Into masterful creations; an artist was born.

What I really loved most were the mountains all 'round,
They were topped off with snow, like soft fluffy mounds.

When the moon was out full, I just couldn't speak,
As it perched just above a majestic white peak.

By staying outside under the moon,
I'd forget the bad people that crowded that room.

The Treasure Fountain

The city is a place to wander and explore
I'd visit the fountain across from the stores.

The fountain squirted high umbrellas of spray,
When the weather was warm, I'd splash and I'd play.

The best part by far, in the water below,
Were the many round coins made of silver and gold.

The silver ones sparkled, the water was cool,
I watched as they sank to the base of the pool.

I wondered why people threw money away.
Was it put there for me, could I spend it today?

With a quick look around, I decided right then,
I would take more than one; yes, I would take ten!

My hands full of coins, a smile on my face,
I hurried away to the store, now in haste!

I found what I wanted; I knew why I came,
Friends for my bathtub, to play bathtub games.

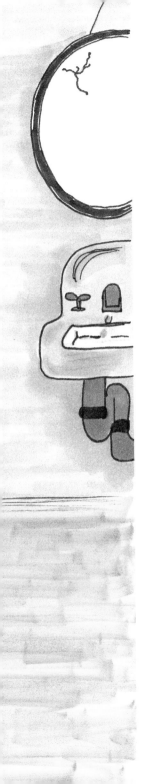

As I gave her my coins, the clerk smiled at me,
"Have fun with your toys; quite a collection I see!"

Turtle, duck, frog, in a blue shopping bag;
I carried them home, and I took off the tags.

The bathroom was empty, how pleased this made me.
I could lock the door tight; no one had a key!

My skin, how it wrinkled, water spilled on the floor.
Some people got mad, and knocked on the door.

I knew they'd want in, but I wasn't ready to leave
I yelled back at them, "Go away, let me be!"

This bathroom so rough, with its peeling old paint,
Kept me safe from Mom's rage, and the men that she'd date.

If it weren't for these moments I found in this place
I wouldn't have dreamed that someday I'd feel safe.

The Orange Float

I remember the day I looked in the sweet shop,
On the wall was a picture: an orange soda pop.

But oh no, not just soda, there was white ice cream too,
In a tall glistening glass, with a cherry and spoon.

I wondered how this would taste on my tongue,
Then I thought to myself, "I just have to have one!"

My pockets were empty, but how I did hope,
That there was some way I could get my own float.

The waitress came over and welcomed me there,
"Hello sugar pie, pull up a chair!"

She brought me an orange float with a big fat white straw.
When I took my first sip, my mouth was in awe.

I drank and I sipped, then my bubble did burst,
My fingers did shake, this was the worst.

No money, still none, time to make an escape,
I took off so fast, please give me a break!

I dashed around the corner, and what happened next?
I was stopped by a man with a badge on his chest.

A policeman? Oh no, I had nothing to say,
How did I get in such trouble today?

The waitress came next, she didn't look pleased,
"Where is my money? Did you steal from me?"

They made me go home to face my mom's scorn.
I knew I was wrong, but I was so torn.

That float was so good, but the slap it was not,
So I hugged Panda tight, and crawled back to my spot.

The Christmas Window

The seasons would change; I would look all around,
To see people dressed warmly, shopping all over town.

I guessed it was Christmas, a busy time of year;
Decorations were hung; there was lots of good cheer.

The windows, they shone with glitter and gold.
The presents displayed were beautiful and bold.

I'd stand on my toes, peek at all I could see,
And imagine those presents were put there for me.

Would Santa come find me, was he coming soon?
Was it true that his reindeer could find every small room?

The glass felt so cold as I pressed my nose tight,
I felt so far away from those Christmas delights.

It was then I decided that I would believe,
One day I'd have presents and a big Christmas tree.

My hands got too cold; there would soon be a storm.
As I walked down the alley, my hope kept me warm.

I Love Grandma

Here's a story of Grandma; she's special to me.
She gave me much more than my mom did, you see.

She'd come and she'd take me away from Mom's place.
I love to remember her most beautiful face.

My grandma, she loved me the best that she could,
She knew there were days when my life was not good.

I cherished those times and her love made me see
That I was worth loving, I felt loved indeed!

We would go to her hotel where she'd give me a bath,
Then she'd comb my wet hair; I'd feel clean at last.

Her tender old arms would hold me so tight,
And I'd soak up her touch, all through the night.

Stanley Park was a favourite place we would go;
We would watch in delight while the squirrels gave a show.

I loved to see Grandma laughing at these
Cute little tricksters, climbing over the trees.

My love was so big I had to thank her some way.
If I captured a squirrel, maybe I could stay.

Now those creatures are saucy, and quick as can be.
I scrambled so quickly to grab one off the tree.

All at once, his full tail was in my little hand,
I thought that I had him! Then he made me so mad.

He scratched and he chattered and he jumped away fast,
Then that crazy black squirrel ran away through the grass.

My grandma she soothed me and kissed my scratched hand,
But mostly she appreciated my clever plan.

"The squirrels have a home as perfect as can be,
And your hugs are enough dear, enough dear for me!"

When Grandma took me home, I didn't want to go.
But she couldn't take me with her, Grandpa said no.

My First Days at School

We left the big city, suitcases in hand;
We moved to Penticton, 'cause Mom met a man.

This man was named Ovey; he had a small place.
He made room for us both and welcomed us to his space.

It was time to start school; I was excited that day.
Would I wear some new clothes, and make friends who would play?

But as I expected there were no clothes with tags,
Just a lunch my mom made, and stuffed in a bag.

I went off alone, found my way to the school,
Just me, my bagged lunch, and my old tattered shoes.

I was just six years old, on the street all alone.
I thought I was big, walking to school on my own,

I arrived just in time to find my small desk.
My teacher, she smiled, and gave us our first test.

It wasn't long before the recess bell went,
So I ran to the playground, that's where we were sent.

I stood watching and waiting, would a friend come my way?
But recess was over; no one came to play.

A few children pushed by me on their way back to class,
They were laughing and pointing, I couldn't pass!

"You have funny front teeth, that stick out really bad,
And you wear funny clothes that look pretty sad!"

My stomach felt sick, but at lunch more was said,
Some kids noticed my sandwich, made with yucky brown bread.

They pinched up their noses as they smelled bacon fat
Mom had smeared on my bread then folded it flat.

As the day came to a close and I wandered off home,
My feet were so heavy and my heart was a stone.

I was confused every day, the kids were unkind.
Had I done something wrong? Was this all I'd find?

A girl threw a rock; it hit me right on the mouth,
I bled all the way home, all the way to my house.

A boy pushed me into a shrub covered in thorns
I cried to Mom; she gave nothing but scorn.

She tugged and she pulled till each prickle came out,
She said I was stupid, and she knocked me about.

Oh, how I'd wished things would be better this time
When we moved to Penticton, I'd hoped life would be fine.

I still felt unloved; I was just in the way.
Mom couldn't care less; what else could I say?

All I'd wanted was friends, and to like my new school.
All I'd got was a lesson on how kids could be cruel.

Cottontail

I recall there were times I'd be sick for too long,
So Mom fed me her pills, pills too big and too strong.

Earaches and body aches were simply ignored
By a mom who was high in her own little world.

I remember how Ovey cared more than most men;
He had a sweet bunny, my Cottontail friend.

I would lay down my head on her soft downy fur;
She would ease up my pain as I lay upon her.

Cottontail, like Panda, gave me comfort some days;
I'm thankful for this gift that somehow found its way.

The Lady at the Church

One day in Penticton, I was wandering free,
When I came to a church with some flowering trees.

A lady was digging, planting seeds in the dirt.
She smiled, and asked, "Will you come into the church?"

She offered me cookies and milk in a glass;
As we chatted awhile, there were questions she asked.

"Do you live around here? Is there anything you need?"
She had some used clothes, they'd fit perfect on me.

She kindly invited me to church that next day,
If I wanted to come, I could learn how to pray.

"In Sunday school," she said, "there are fun things to do.
If you want to learn about God, they do that here too."

On Sunday I loved the time I spent there,
I sang songs about God, and they taught me He cared.

I could ask Him to help me when hurts came my way,
I could tell Him I'm tired, alone, and afraid.

My Sunday school friends said God really loved me,
I could ask him to promise that He'd never leave.

A Birthday for Me

It went downhill with Ovey; there were fights all the time,
So Mom moved in with Jack, and said, "It will be fine."

His character was friendly, and I liked him a lot,
My mom seemed so different, happier I thought!

For my birthday Jack honoured and treated me kind
With a rose-covered cake and gifts wrapped in twine!

New stuffies to cuddle and balloons to watch float
He topped it all off and gave me a Coke!

It fizzed and it bubbled, and snuck up my nose;
An awesome first birthday — I never had one, you know!

Christmas came too, with a tree and more gifts,
I couldn't believe people lived life like this.

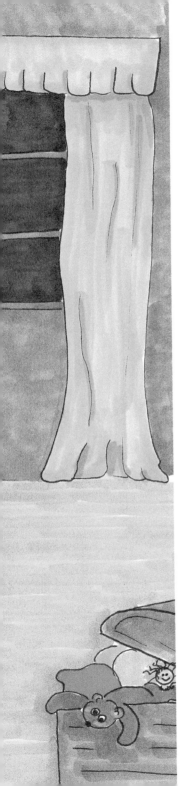

My First Friend

Jack moved us to Princeton; we found a new space.
I was lucky to find a friend in this unlikely place.

Her name was Sally; we met on the bus.
We hung out at school and became special buds.

I liked her a lot; she lived right down the street.
As my very first friend; she was very sweet.

Days would go by; Jack and Mom disappeared.
In the evenings I needed someone else to be near.

I'd run over to Sally's, or to her grandpa's house,
I was welcomed and cared for without any fuss.

There were cookies and Barbies, and laughter and more;
These neighbours were welcoming, wonderful, and warm.

In a memory I cherish Sally saw I was cold,
She went up to her closet, and brought down a load

Of boots and a coat. I could hardly believe
My dear caring friend giving these things to me!

All that winter I smiled as I cuddled up in that coat,
My feet were all snug; I was filled with such hope!

Sally's grandpa was special, we'd visit his place,
We'd run and we'd play in the big, open space.

He had a Ford truck; it was red, it was loud.
He would take us for trips all the way downtown.

He'd give us some money; we'd buy fries and a cone.
What a treat for us girls, we'd eat all the way home.

This whole family was loving, but they just couldn't believe,
How my mother would treat me; how she'd just simply leave.

They cared while they could; they poured love over me.
With these people I learned what true family could be!

Each time I went home, I left with a smile;
Being with Sally's sweet family made me forget for a while.

The Cabin

As all my tales go, things at home got real bad.
Mom started to drink; she would yell and get mad!

The screaming would start as she and Jack fought!
I would hide in my corner, covered my ears quite a lot!

Soon Jack kicked us out, we had not a cent.
With our suitcases in hand, no money for rent.

My young heart was anxious, but I had no voice,
I followed my mother; she gave me no choice.

So far from my friend, I had nowhere to run.
This shack where we moved to would not be much fun.

This new place was eerie, the worst one by far:
A dark little cabin, in the woods, with no car.

I was often hungry, our groceries were few
But a hunter brought meat, such kindness was new.

Raw meat would stay raw, for there wasn't a stove.
My mom couldn't cook, so the meat it got old.

I'd find stale bread, and wipe off the dirt,
It was this that I'd eat, when my stomach would hurt.

Mom ignored bills, and the wind whistled through,
The cabin grew chilly, and my lips, they turned blue.

There was an old heater; some days it gave heat,
Then I cuddled in close, and curled up my feet.

But Jack still loved Mom, he'd come get her sometimes,
And they'd leave me for days; this was not fine.

As I tell my sad story, please don't feel bad.
For some days I'd find joy and find myself glad.

One day I found kittens under the stairs,
They were tiny and hungry, alone and so scare

My cabin seemed perfect to house these lost souls,
We'd snuggle and play, they'd tickle my toes.

They skittered and scampered; we played out the day.
My mom would complain; I kept them out of her way.

Soon I had 13 of these grey furry friends,
These cats would get sassy, the meowing didn't end!

When Jack and Mom left, not caring about me,
It was just me and my cats, such sweet company.

The cabin smelled bad, with the dirt, and the pee,
My mom didn't notice, she just ignored me.

One day she got sick and stayed in her room.
I knew things could get worse, if she didn't wake soon!

Someone called for an ambulance, I don't know who.
I was left all alone, not sure what to do.

A neighbour heard the siren, and saw my bare feet.
I had to stay with her a while, at least I would eat.

When my mom was better, Jack came to find me.
When he took me back home, he smelled the poo and the pee!

He screamed and he shouted, "Just look at this place!
You clean it up now, Squeaks!" He slapped my small face.

"Your mom will be home soon; get down on your knees.
This house smells like rot; start scrubbing it clean!"

I said goodbye to my cats as Jack carried them out,
They were not going to live; I had no doubt.

After all that, Mom thought it best that we move,
So we packed up our stuff and found an old hotel room.

How long would we stay? It was so hard to tell;
I held hope close, and wished all would be well.

Finding My Way

Back in Penticton at a seedy hotel,
Mom got a bit better, but never seemed well.

This life of uncertainty and Mom's cruel ways,
Made me want to lash out and cry every day!

I'd wander round town to distract me from her,
But my soul seemed so raw, and my days were a blur.

One day as I walked, I seemed to be drawn,
To that sweet little church I had once come upon.

As I knocked, I wondered, was that lady still there?
Then I saw her bright smile, and with relief I just stared!

She was happy to see me; she took my small hand.
We shared more milk and cookies as if this meeting was planned.

I told her my story with a great many tears.
It was then that she said, "Don't give up, my sweet dear!

God's provided His people; you may not see it now.
But one day you'll know why and one day you'll see how.

They were placed in your life to bring kindness and love
They were sent by our Father, our Father above."

I walked away peaceful, my heart seemed content.
I felt a new strength; I understood what she meant.

I could keep going on; I could face each new day
Knowing somehow that hope was guiding my way.

Laura Looks Back

As I think of it now, it isn't hard to believe,
That in those hard days, people cared about me.

There were no words back then to explain the good days,
When I felt safe and loved, and found joy in small ways.

The small kindnesses I felt, affected me somehow,
I now know it was hope, that's what carries me now.

Without those precious people, I don't know who I'd be.
I'm so thankful they showed that they cared for me.

So when you read this book, please understand,
God is thinking of you, and He has a great plan.

He is using his people, placing them in your life.
If you look really hard, you'll see that I'm right.

You are a child of a God; He knows all that you do.
He wants to protect you, and carry you through.

The pain and the hurting, the sorrow and shame,
Can be given to Him, 'cause his promise remains.

He will care for you always; nothing you do,
Could take his love away. He'll be there for you.

Just so you know: my life got better by far.
At times it was difficult, and the road, very hard.

I am blessed with four children, grandchildren make more.
I smiled, I survived, 'cause hope opened the door.

Thank you for coming on this journey with me;
I am praying for you, child, that one day you'll be free.

Sharing Time

Questions to consider when leading and guiding
the child into meaningful Conversation.

1. Have you ever had a problem that made you feel very sad? What did you do to make the problem a little better?

2. Squeaks has some special friends including Panda, the pigeons, Grandma, and Sally in her life to give her comfort and hope. Who are the special friends in your life that help you feel happy and safe?

3. Think of your body. What does your body feel like when you are safe? What does your body feel like when you are not safe?

4. Think about a time when someone was really kind to you. How did they help you? What did they say? How did that make you feel?

5. Can you think of a time when you were kind and caring to others? What happened?

6. Do you know someone who might need your kindness? What could you do?

7. Think about a happy memory that you always keep warm in your heart. Tell me about this memory.

8. When something bad happens to you, does this mean that you are bad?

9. If you could talk to Squeaks, what would you tell her when something bad happens in her life?

10. Do you think Squeaks ever gives up hoping things would get better? How could we remind Squeaks that she is cared about and that she is not alone?

11. The squirrel poem is a fun story about how much Squeaks wants to show love to her grandma. Is there someone you want to show love and thankfulness to? How could you show your love and thankfulness to this person?

12. What is your favourite story about Squeaks? Why?

A little about
the Author and Illustrator of
Hide and Squeaks

Leslie is a Preschool Teacher who loves writing songs and poems. She is thrilled to use her gift of words to help Laura share her story with young children everywhere. Lucy has always loved being creative with her artwork and photography. She enjoys beauty all around her and is honoured to be able to help bring Laura's story to life. Lucy and Leslie, who both reside in the Fraser Valley, have been friends for over 20 years.

Tellwell Talent • www.tellwell.ca

ISBN 978-1-77302-608-4 (Hardcover)

CPSIA information can be obtained
at www.ICGtesting.com
Printed in the USA
LVOW05*1915160917
548954LV00002B/3/P